A Guide for Using

The Mitten

in the Classroom

Based on the book written by **Jan Brett**

This guide was written by **Mary R**

Teacher Created Resources, Inc.
6421 Industry Way
Westminster, CA 92683
www.teachercreated.com
ISBN: 978-1-57690-627-9
©2000 Teacher Created Resources, Inc.
Reprinted, 2008
Made in U.S.A.

Edited by
Mary Kaye Taggart
Illustrated by
Wendi Wright-Davis
Cover Art by
Sue Fullam

Table of Contents

Introduction

A good book can touch the lives of children like a good friend. Young minds can turn to literary treasures for companionship, recreation, comfort, and guidance. They can be inspired by the pictures, words, and characters. Great care has been taken in selecting the books and unit activities that comprise the primary series of Literature Units. Teachers who use this literature unit to supplement their own valuable ideas can follow one of the methods below.

Sample Lesson Plan

The Sample Lesson Plan on page 4 provides you with a specific set of lesson plan suggestions for *The Mitten*. Each of the lessons can take from one to several days to complete and can include all or some of the suggested activities. Refer to the Suggestions for Using the Unit Activities on pages 7–9 for more information relating to the unit activities.

Unit Planner

If you wish to tailor the suggestions on page 4 to a format other than that prescribed in the Sample Lesson Plan, a blank Unit Planner is provided on page 5. On a specific day, you may choose the activities that you wish to include by writing the activity number or a brief notation about the lesson in the Unit Activities section. Space has also been provided for reminders, comments, and other pertinent information relating to each day's activities. Reproduce copies of the Unit Planner as needed.

Sample Lesson Plan

Lesson 1

- Read *The Mitten* by Jan Brett.
- Read aloud Getting to Know the Book and the Author (page 6).
- As a whole class, complete the Story Map (page 19).
- Discuss the Animal Picture and Word Cards (pages 16 and 17).
- Complete the pattern activity (pages 27 and 28).
- Make a graph of the students' favorite mitten colors (page 30).

Lesson 2

- Reread *The Mitten* by Jan Brett.
- Ask the Story Questions based on Bloom's Taxonomy (page 15).
- Use the Sentence Strip Frames (page 14) to complete some pocket chart activities (pages 11–13).
- Do the Animal Logic Problems (pages 25–27).
- Select one of the Mitten Math Activities (pages 30–34).
- Make the Animals of Ukraine minibook (pages 42–44).

Lesson 3

- Read *The Mitten* by Alvin Tresselt.
- Complete a row in the Comparing Stories activity (page 20).
- Do the Winter Days activity (page 29).
- Complete the Mitten Measuring activity (page 35).
- Begin practicing the Readers' Theater script (pages 45–47).

Lesson 4

- Read *The Old Man's Mitten*: *A Ukrainian Tale* by Yevonne Pollock.
- Complete a row in the Comparing Stories activity (page 20).
- Read aloud the information on Ukraine (page 39) and do the map activity (pages 40 and 41).

- Do the Before, in the Middle, and After math activity (page 32).
- Practice the Readers' Theater script (pages 45–47).

Lesson 5

- Read *The Mitten* by Tom Botting.
- Complete a row in the Comparing Stories activity (page 20).
- Do the Skip Counting by Twos, Fives, and Tens activity (page 33).
- Practice the Readers' Theater script (pages 45–47).

Lesson 6

- Read *One Snowy Night* by Nick Butterworth.
- Complete a row in the Comparing Stories activity (page 20).
- Do How Much Is Each Name Worth? (pages 23 and 24).
- Practice the Readers' Theater script (pages 45–47).

Lesson 7

- Read *Who's That Knocking at My Door?* by Reinhard Michl.
- Complete a row in the Comparing Stories activity (page 20).
- Do How Many Cubes Will Fit into Your Mitten? (page 36).
- Practice the Readers' Theater script (pages 45–47).

Lesson 8

- Read *The Woodcutter's Mitten* by Loek Koopmans.
- Complete a row in the Comparing Stories activity (page 20).
- Complete the Pairs of Mittens activity (page 33).
- Practice the Readers' Theater script (pages 45–47).

Unit Planner

Unit Activities

Date:

Notes:

Unit Activities

Date:

Notes:

Unit Activities

Date:

Notes:

Unit Activities

Date:

Notes:

Unit Activities

Date:

Notes:

Unit Activities

Date:

Notes:

Getting to Know the Book and the Author

About the Book

(The Mitten *is published in the United States from Putnam Publishing Group, 1996. It is also available in Canada from Philomel, Price Stern Sloan, in UK from BeJo Sales, and in AUS from Warner International.*)

The Mitten is an old Ukrainian folktale retold with beautiful illustrations by Jan Brett. There are many versions of this story. Brett chose a little boy to be the main character in her version, and she used her imagination to make up her own details.

The Mitten is about a young boy named Nicki, who receives two handmade, white mittens from his grandmother. One wintry day he drops one of his mittens in the snow. Unbeknownst to Nicki, forest animals move into the mitten for warmth. The animals range in size from a small mouse to a large bear! It is delightful and amazing to see how the mitten stretches to an extraordinary size in order to hold all of the animals.

About the Author

Jan Brett was born on December 1, 1949, in Hingham, Massachusetts. She began drawing at an early age. By the age of six, Jan Brett knew she wanted to be an illustrator of children's books.

In her childhood, Brett often retreated into the pages of beautiful picture books and dreamed of becoming an illustrator. "I used to always fantasize about being left on a desert island so I could draw all the time," she once said in an interview with Scholastic Books. She continues, "I remember the special quiet of rainy days when I felt that I could enter the pages of my beautiful picture books. Now I try to recreate that feeling of believing that the imaginary place I'm drawing really exists. The detail in my work helps to convince me, and I hope others as well, that such places might be real."

Jan Brett attended Colby Junior College from 1968–1969 and the Boston Museum of Fine Arts School in 1970. Her first book *Fritz and the Beautiful Horses* was published in 1981. Jan Brett did both the writing and the illustrating for this book.

To retell the story of *The Mitten*, Jan Brett visited the Ukrainian section of New York City to find out more about the Ukrainian culture. She visited the Ukrainian Museum and corresponded with many people from Ukraine. She also enlisted the help of Oxana Piaseckyj, a Ukrainian woman who helped Jan Brett by translating different versions of *The Mitten* into English.

Brett says her favorite book is whichever one she is currently working on because she feels most like herself when she is drawing. It is easy to see that Brett loves what she does because each of her books reflects her unwavering attention to detail and passion for authenticity. Jan Brett infuses her books with the painstaking care of a master artisan.

Jan Brett loves to illustrate the borders of the pages of her books with detailed drawings. The border drawings in *The Mitten* show what Nicki is doing as the mitten is filling up with animals. It takes her one hour to do one inch of drawing and months to complete an entire book!

Jan Brett lives with her husband in Norwell, Massachusetts. You can contact her through her Web page at *www.janbrett.com*.

Suggestions for Using the Unit Activities

Use some or all of the following suggestions to help the children understand and appreciate the story as well as to introduce, reinforce, and extend skills across the curriculum. The suggested activities have been divided up by subject to assist the teacher in planning the literature unit.

Language Arts

- Reproduce page 10. Before completing activity 1 on page 11, review with students the words listed on the page. (*Page 10 answers:* glinty—dull, snug—loose, quickly— slowly, warm—cold, drowsy—wakeful, plump—flat, swelled—shrank, enormous—tiny)

- Prepare in advance the mitten- and yarn-shaped vocabulary cards (page 13), the sentence strips (page 14), and the question cards (page 15) according to the directions on pages 11 and 12. Laminate the cards and cut them apart. Place them in the pocket chart when you are ready to use them.

- Photocopy the Animal Picture and Word Cards (pages 16 and 17) onto construction paper. Color the picture cards. Laminate all of the cards to ensure durability. The students can use the cards to practice matching each animal name to its picture.

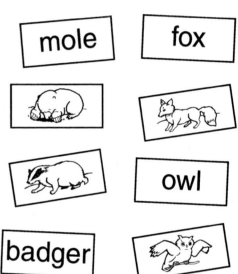

- Photocopy two sets of the Animal Picture and Word Cards (pages 16 and 17). Laminate the sets of cards for playing Concentration. Before beginning the game, determine whether the players will be trying to find two cards that match exactly (the same pictures or the same names) or will be looking for pairs of matching name and picture cards. These cards can be placed in a center to give the students additional practice in recognizing the animal names and pictures.

- Enlarge the Animal Picture and Word Cards (pages 16 and 17) to make stick puppets for the Readers' Theater script (pages 45–47). The students can color the enlarged pictures, mount them on craft sticks or on 2" x 10" (5 cm x 25 cm) pieces of heavy card stock, and use them as props during the Readers' Theater presentation.

- Each day, select one of the Journal Writing Topics (page 18) for the students to use as a prompt. First, brainstorm ideas about the selected topic as a whole class. The students can write individually, with a partner, with a small group, or as a whole class on the topic.

- The Story Map (page 19) can be used to help the students organize their thoughts about *The Mitten* by Jan Brett or any other stories on the mitten theme.

- Comparing Stories (page 20) is a great way for the whole class to organize information about each version of *The Mitten* that is read. The Comparing Stories page can be used as an overhead, or it can be enlarged on a piece of butcher paper to record the information.

- The Mitten Chants and Songs (page 21) can be rewritten onto large pieces of chart paper and placed on a chart stand from which the whole class can read. They can also be photocopied and made into a Mitten Chants and Songs booklet for each student.

Suggestions for Using the Unit Activities *(cont.)*

Math

- Each day, select a different math journal question (page 22). Photocopy a class set of the questions and cut them apart. Give each of the students a strip with that day's question on it. The students can glue the strips into their math journals and draw pictures below them to help solve the questions. They can then write short math sentences for the problems and their answers.

- Photocopy How Much Is Each Name Worth? (pages 23 and 24) for the students. The students can use the paper money and the alphabet price code to figure out the "value" of each animal's name. Extend this activity to find out the values of other words. To do this, cut sentence strips into 6" (15 cm) lengths. Write words from the book, the months of the year, days of the week, students' first or last names, etc., on the strips. Pass out the strips, one to each student. Tell the students to figure out the values of their words by gluing the appropriate paper coins above each letter in the words and then adding up all of the coins.

- Make copies of the pictures on page 27. Give each student a strip of the pictures. Ask them to cut their strips into six individual squares. As you read the Animal Logic Problems (pages 25 and 26) aloud, have the students place the animals in the correct order on their desks. To extend this activity, have the students develop their own logic problems and share them either verbally or in written form with the class.

- Make a copy of page 27 for each student. Also make a copy of the Animal Pattern Pocket (page 28) on construction paper for each student. Show the students how to assemble the pattern pockets. Tell them to cut apart the animal pictures and use the squares to make patterns. (The students may wish to use letters or numbers to label their patterns. For example: ABCABC or 123123) Have them store their pictures in the pockets they made. Repeat the activity later in the unit, or the students may practice their pattern-making skills in their free time.

- The Winter Days activity sheet (page 29) requires the students to look at a calendar for information. Make a master copy of this page and either fill in the name of the month and dates before photocopying or have the students do it after the page has been photocopied. The questions should be based upon the month and dates used in the calendar.

- For detailed instructions of math activities which use the Mitten Number Board on page 37 and the Mitten Patterns on page 38, refer to pages 30–34.

Answer Key for Pages 25 and 26

Four Characters

  A. bear, mouse, owl, mole

  B. owl, bear, mole, mouse

  C. mole, bear, mouse, owl

  D. mouse, owl, mole, bear

  E. mouse, owl, bear, mole

Five Characters

  A. bear, rabbit, mouse, mole, owl

  B. mouse, owl, mole, rabbit, bear

  C. rabbit, bear, mouse, owl, mole

  D. owl, mole, rabbit, bear, mouse

  E. mole, mouse, rabbit, owl, bear

Six Characters

  A. mouse, owl, mole, rabbit, fox, bear

  B. fox, mole, mouse, rabbit, owl, bear

  C. owl, mole, rabbit, fox, bear, mouse

  D. rabbit, fox, bear, mouse, owl, mole

Suggestions for Using the Unit Activities *(cont.)*

Social Studies

- Page 39 provides background information on the Ukraine. This information can be read aloud to the students.

- Make a copy of pages 40 and 41, Map of Ukraine, for each student. If you are doing this activity as a whole class, an overhead projection copy can also be made. This page provides geographical information about Ukraine and its surrounding countries.

Science

- All of the animals in Jan Brett's retelling of *The Mitten* can be found living and thriving in Ukraine. Photocopy a set of pages 42–44, Animals of Ukraine, for each student. Also make copies of the animal pictures on pages 16 and 17 for each student. To assemble, the students need to cut the book's pages apart on the dashed lines and then staple the pages together. Finally, the students glue the appropriate picture on each page.

- After they have completed their books, ask the students the follow-up questions at the bottom of page 39.

Culminating Activity

- The Readers' Theater script (pages 45–47) can be presented to both the students' parents and to other classes. Depending upon the size of your class, the students can be divided into two or three casts. This will insure that all of the students will have a part. For props, enlarge the animal pictures on pages 16 and 17. For the mittens, cut one pair of mittens that are the same size out of white construction paper (or use real mittens) and cut a single, extremely large mitten out of white construction paper. For Baba, make a wig out of yarn and provide a ball of yarn and knitting needles to use as props. The actor or actress who plays Nicki can wear the white mittens and a winter cap.

Vocabulary Word List

Directions: Match each word from the story (in the left mitten) to the word that has the opposite meaning (in the right mitten). Write each pair of opposite words on the mittens below.

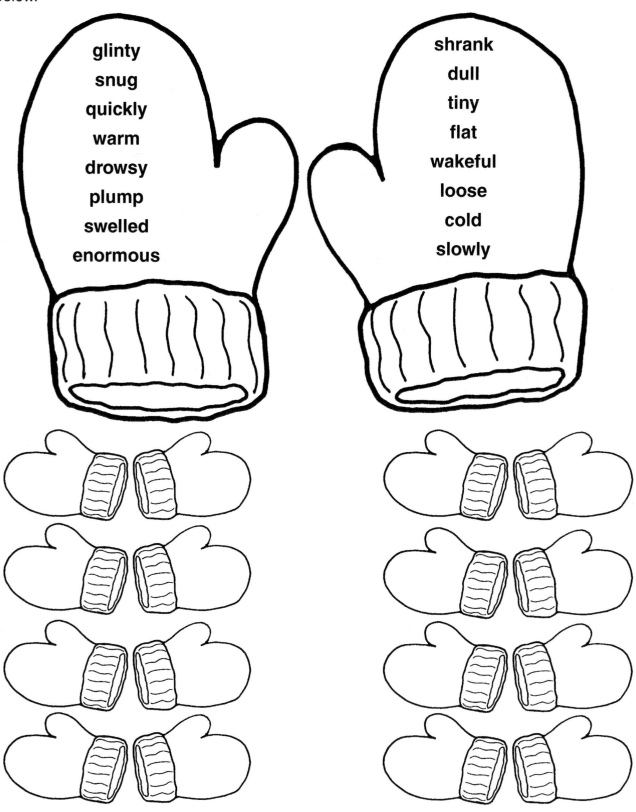

glinty
snug
quickly
warm
drowsy
plump
swelled
enormous

shrank
dull
tiny
flat
wakeful
loose
cold
slowly

10

Pocket Chart Activities

Prepare a pocket chart for sorting and using the vocabulary cards, animal picture and name cards, story question cards, and sentence strips.

How to Make a Pocket Chart

If a commercial one is unavailable, you can make a pocket chart if you have access to a laminator. Begin by laminating a 24" x 36" (61 cm x 91 cm) piece of colored tagboard. Run about 20" (51 cm) of additional plastic. To make nine pockets, cut the clear plastic into nine equal strips. Space the strips equally down the 36" (91 cm) length of the tagboard. Attach each strip with cellophane tape along the bottom and sides. This will hold the sentence strips, word cards, etc., and it can be displayed in a learning center or mounted on a chalk tray for use with a group. A sample chart is illustrated below.

Chart Racks

An inexpensive chart rack can be purchased at most local discount retailers. Purchase a garment rack, and attach the pocket chart to it by using "O" rings. If you rewrite the chants and songs (page 21) onto chart paper, they can also be put on "O" rings and hung from the garment rack.

How to Use the Pocket Chart

---

1. Photocopy the mitten and yarn patterns from page 13 onto card stock or construction paper. Write the vocabulary words from the story on the mitten shapes. Write their opposite words on the yarn shapes. Laminate both sets of words. Place the mitten words in the pocket chart and have the students place the opposite words next to the appropriate words.

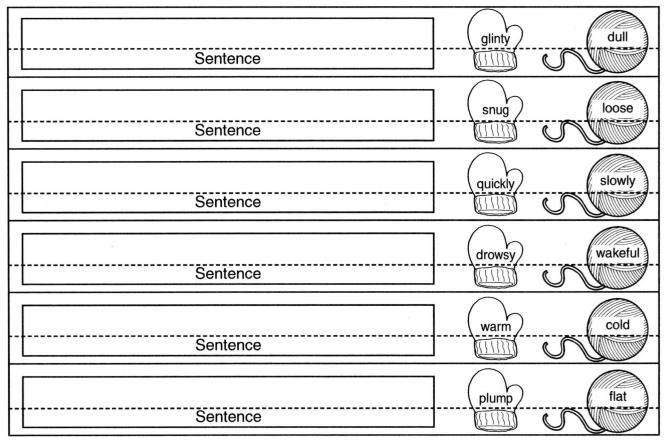

Pocket Chart Activities *(cont.)*

How to Use the Pocket Chart *(cont.)*

---

2. Make enlarged copies of the blank sentence strips on page 14. Write simple sentences about the main events of the story on the blank sentence strips. Laminate the strips for durability. Mix up the order of the strips and ask the students to place them in the correct sequential order in the pocket chart.

3. Help the students practice their oral reading skills by reading out loud the sentence strips you created in activity 1 on page 11.

4. Make enlarged copies of the words and pictures on pages 16 and 17. Color the pictures, and laminate both the words and the pictures. Place the animal pictures in the pocket chart, and have the students match the words to the correct pictures.

5. Reproduce the mitten pattern from page 13 onto six different colors of construction paper. (Make several of each color.) Use a different paper color to represent each of Bloom's Levels of Learning.

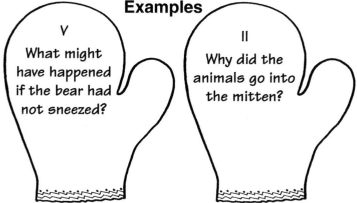

Examples

V
What might have happened if the bear had not sneezed?

II
Why did the animals go into the mitten?

I.   **Knowledge—red**

II. **Comprehension—orange**

III. **Application—yellow**

IV. **Analysis—green**

V.   **Synthesis—blue**

VI. **Evaluation—purple**

Write a story question from page 15 on the appropriate color-coded mitten pattern. Write the level of the question and the question on the mitten, as shown in the example above. As each question is asked, place the question in the pocket chart. These cards will provide the opportunity for the students to develop and practice higher-level critical thinking skills. The cards can be used with some or all of the following activities:

• Use a specific color-coded set of cards to question students at a particular level of learning.

• Have a child choose a card and read it aloud or give it to the teacher to read aloud. The child may answer the question or call on a volunteer to answer it.

• Pair the students. The teacher reads a question. Partners take turns responding to the question.

• Play a game. Divide the class into teams. Ask for a response to a question written on one of the question cards. Teams score a point for each appropriate response.

6. Make copies of the small mitten patterns (page 38) onto construction paper. Number the mittens 0–100 and laminate them. Once the mittens have been cut out, place them in the pocket chart. These mittens are then ready to use for practicing numerical order, skip counting, and working with numbers to 100 (see pages 32 and 33).

Pocket Chart Patterns

Teacher Note: *See pages 11 and 12 for directions.*

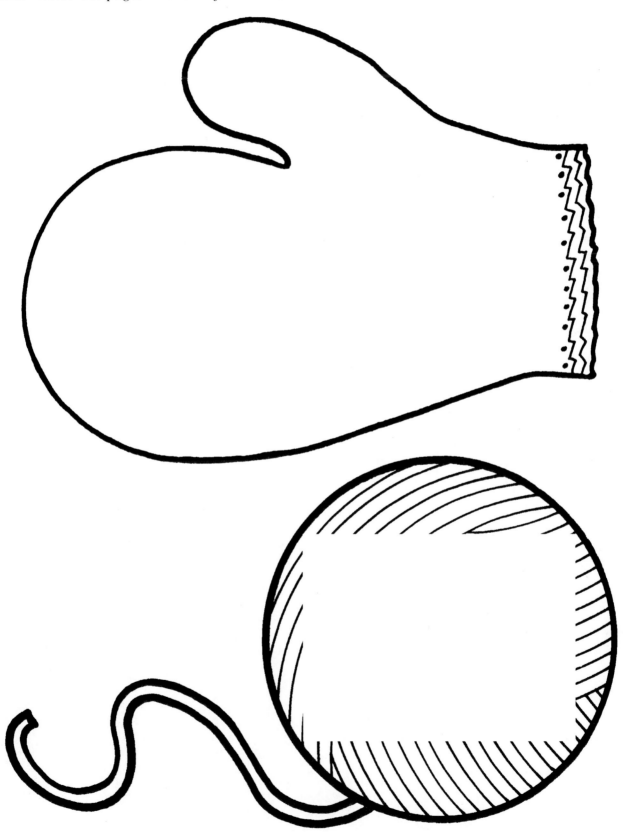

Sentence Strip Frames

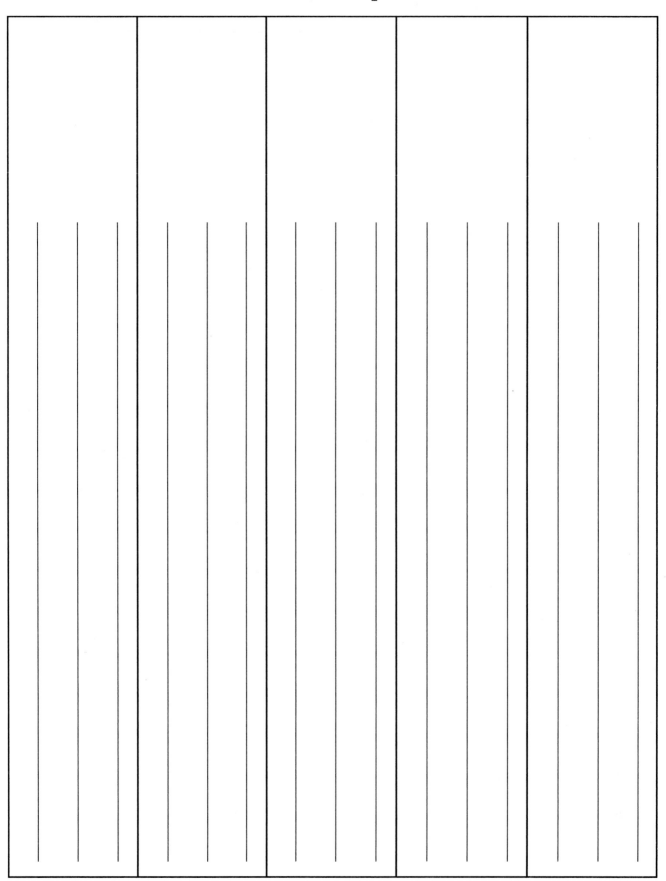

Story Questions

Use the following questions with the suggested activities on page 12.

I. Knowledge *(ability to recall information)*

- How many animals went into the mitten?
- Name the animals that went into the mitten.
- What color was the mitten?
- Who made the mittens?
- What was the boy's name?

II. Comprehension *(basic understanding of information)*

- Why did the animals go into the mitten?
- Why was Nicki's mitten so big at the end of the story?
- Retell or rewrite the beginning, middle, and end of the story.
- At the end of the story, why did Baba look at the pair of mittens so curiously?
- Sequence the story.

III. Application *(ability to do something new with the information)*

- Can you think of any other animals that might like to go into the mitten to get warm?
- Where did the animals go after they left the mitten?
- Where else (besides the mitten) could the animals go to get warm?
- Where would the animals in the story normally like to live?
- Where would you go or what would you do to get warm if you were out in the cold?
- What time of year does it get cold?

IV. Analysis *(ability to examine the parts of a whole)*

- How many different ways could you sort the animals?
- How are the animals alike? How are the animals different?
- What is another animal that is like a hedgehog? a fox? a bear? an owl? a mole? a mouse? a badger? a rabbit?
- Sort the animals by size from smallest to largest.
- Which animals took up the most room in the mitten? Which animals took up the least amount of room in the mitten?

V. Synthesis *(ability to bring together information to make something new)*

- What might have happened if the bear had not sneezed?
- What would the animals need to do if they decided to stay in the mitten?
- What if Nicki had come back and found the mitten with the animals still inside of it?
- Which two animals would get along the best? the worst?
- What would each animal be able to contribute to the group?

VI. Evaluation *(ability to form and defend an opinion)*

- Explain how all of those animals could get into the mitten.
- Is it possible for the animals to live together in harmony? Explain your answer.

Animal Picture and Word Cards

Mole

Rabbit

Hedgehog

Owl

Animal Picture and Word Cards *(cont.)*

	Badger
	Fox
	Bear
	Mouse

Journal Writing Topics

The Mitten is a great story to use to spark students' interest in writing. Here are some writing prompts that you might want to give to your students. Select a prompt and brainstorm with the students a list of ideas related to the topic. The students can write on their own, with a partner, in a group, or even as a whole class!

- If you live in an area where it sometimes snows, are white mittens a good choice? Why or why not?

- Describe the perfect kind of mittens. Of what are they made? What special qualities do they have?

- Why do you think Nicki wanted white mittens?

- How come Nicki did not notice that he had dropped one of the mittens on that cold, wintry day?

- How was it possible for all of the animals to fit into the mitten?

- Many of the animals who went into the mitten to get warm are natural enemies of one another. How come the animals in the mitten never fought with one another? How come none of the animals were ever frightened by one another?

- What would have happened if the mole had not let any of the other animals into the mitten?

- Which animal from the story do you like best? Explain why.

- Which do you like better, mittens or gloves? Tell why you prefer one over the other.

- Using your own words, retell the story of *The Mitten.*

- Write your own version of *The Mitten.* Use characters of your choice, and change the setting.

- Write directions for putting on (or taking off) a pair of mittens. What would you have to do first? next? last?

- Do you think *The Mitten* is a true story? Why or why not?

- Pick one of the animal characters from the story. Describe what the animal's day is like. Where does the animal live? What does it eat? Who are its enemies? Who are its friends?

Story Map

Directions: Use this story map to organize your information about *The Mitten.*

Title

_____
_____

Author

_____
_____

Setting

_____
_____

Characters

_____
_____
_____
_____
_____
_____

The Mitten

Main Event

_____
_____
_____
_____
_____
_____

Problems

_____
_____
_____
_____
_____

Solutions

_____
_____
_____
_____
_____

Comparing Stories

Teacher Note: *See page 7 for ideas on using this page.*

Differences						
Similarities						
Events						
Setting						
Characters						
Title and Author						

Mitten Chants and Songs

"I Love Mittens!"

I love mittens!
Mittens that are big,
Mittens that are small,
Mittens that are tiny—
I love them all!

I love mittens!
Mittens that are red,
Mittens that are blue,
Mittens that are purple,
Mittens of every hue!

I love mittens!
Mittens that are soft,
Mittens that are rough,
Mittens that are bumpy—
I just can't get enough!

I love mittens!

"Mittens"
a chant

Mittens can be red.
Mittens can be orange.
Mittens can be yellow.
Mittens can be green.
Mittens can be blue.
Mittens can be purple.
Mittens can be a rainbow!

"Counting Mittens"
a chant

One mitten, two mittens, three mittens, four,
Five mittens, six mittens, seven mittens,
   more,
Eight mittens, nine mittens, ten mittens
   galore,
We have mittens, mittens by the score!

"Mitten, Mitten"
Sung to the tune of
"Twinkle, Twinkle, Little Star"

Mitten, mitten, where are you?
I have one.
I used to have two.
Up in the hay loft I did check.
Found nothing there
but a stick.
Mitten, mitten, where are you?
I have one.
I used to have two.

"Ten Little Mittens"
Sung to the tune of "Ten Little Indians"

One little, two little, three little mittens,
Four little, five little, six little mittens,
Seven little, eight little, nine little mittens,
Ten little mittens in our class.
Red ones, orange ones, blue ones too,
Brown ones, green ones, pink ones too,
Gray ones, white ones, yellow ones too,
Ten little mittens in our class.

"Have You Ever Seen My Mittens?"
Sung to the tune of
"Have You Ever Seen a Lassie?"

Have you ever seen my mittens?
My mittens? My mittens?
Have you ever seen my mittens?
I dropped them somewhere.
I checked in my pockets.
I checked in my jacket.
Have you ever seen my mittens?
I dropped them somewhere.

Math Journal Questions

Teacher Directions: Read the math journal questions aloud to the whole class or photocopy the questions and cut them apart. Each day, give the class one of the questions. The questions can be written or glued onto a piece of paper or written in a math journal. The students can each draw a picture to help solve the question and then write a short sentence describing the answer. (**Note:** For the last question, have copies of the pictures on pages 16 and 17 available for the students.)

1. In the story, *The Mitten*, eight animals went into the mitten: a badger, a hedgehog, a mole, a bear, a rabbit, an owl, a fox, and a meadow mouse. Altogether, how many legs were there?

2. The eight animals went into the mitten: the badger, the hedgehog, the mole, the bear, the rabbit, the owl, the fox, and the meadow mouse. Altogether, how many tails were there?

3. Each of the eight animals has two eyes. How many eyes are there in all?

4. Snowshoe Rabbit found three mittens while hopping through the forest this morning. He found two more mittens at his home. How many mittens does Snowshoe Rabbit now have?

5. Bear made two mittens. Meadow Mouse made four mittens. Fox made one mitten. How many mittens did they make in all?

6. Badger had three pairs of mittens. Mole ate three of the mittens. How many mittens does Badger have left? (**Hint:** Remember that there are two mittens in each pair.)

7. Baba can knit one pair of mittens in 10 minutes. How many pairs of mittens can Baba knit in 30 minutes?

8. Hedgehog went to the mitten store. He saw 12 pairs of mittens in all. He saw four pairs of green mittens, two pairs of yellow mittens, and some blue mittens. How many pairs of blue mittens did Hedgehog see?

9. Look at pictures of the animals from the story. How many different ways can you sort the animals? (by color? by size? by the number of legs? by fur? by food habits?) Describe how you could sort the animals.

Answers

1. 30 legs	4. 5 mittens	7. 3 pairs
2. 7 tails	5. 7 mittens	8. 6 blue pairs
3. 16 eyes	6. 3 mittens	9. Answers will vary.

How Much Is Each Name Worth?

Directions: Use the Alphabet Price Code (page 24) to find the value of each animal's name.

1. _____ + _____ + _____ + _____ + _____ + _____ + _____ + _____ = _____¢
     H   E   D   G   E   H   O   G

2. _____ + _____ + _____ + _____ + _____ + _____ = _____¢
     B   A   D   G   E   R

3. _____ + _____ + _____ + _____ = _____¢
     B   E   A   R

4. _____ + _____ + _____ + _____ + _____ + _____ = _____¢
     R   A   B   B   I   T

5. _____ + _____ + _____ = _____¢
     O   W   L

6. _____ + _____ + _____ = _____¢
     F   O   X

7. _____ + _____ + _____ + _____ + _____ = _____¢
     M   O   U   S   E

8. _____ + _____ + _____ + _____ = _____¢
     M   O   L   E

Teacher Note: Fold before reproducing this page.

Answers: **1.** 34¢ **2.** 28¢ **3.** 22¢ **4.** 19¢ **5.** 25¢ **6.** 25¢ **7.** 22¢ **8.** 26¢

How Much Is Each Name Worth? *(cont.)*

Directions: Use the following code to figure out how much the animal names on page 23 are worth. Cut out the coins at the bottom of the page to help you calculate the answers.

Alphabet Price Code

A = 1¢	G = 1¢	N = 1¢	U = 5¢
B = 1¢	H = 1¢	O = 5¢	V = 5¢
C = 5¢	I = 5¢	P = 5¢	W = 10¢
D = 5¢	J = 5¢	Q = 10¢	X = 10¢
E = 10¢	K = 10¢	R = 10¢	Y = 1¢
F = 10¢	L = 10¢	S = 1¢	Z = 1¢
	M = 1¢	T = 1¢	

Animal Logic Problems

Teacher Note: *See page 8 for directions and answers to this activity.*

These problems use four of the animal characters.

A • The bear went into the mitten first.
- The mouse went into the mitten second.
- The owl went into the mitten third.
- The mole went into the mitten fourth.

B • The owl went into the mitten first.
- The bear went into the mitten second.
- The mole went into the mitten third.
- The mouse went into the mitten fourth.

C • The mole went into the mitten first.
- The bear went into the mitten second.
- The mouse went into the mitten third.
- The owl went into the mitten fourth.

D • The mouse went into the mitten first.
- The owl went into the mitten second.
- The mole went into the mitten third.
- The bear went into the mitten fourth.

E • The bear went into the mitten third.
- The owl went into the mitten second.
- The mouse went into the mitten first.
- The mole went into the mitten fourth.

These problems use five of the animal characters.

A • The bear went into the mitten first.
- The mouse went into the mitten third.
- The rabbit went into the mitten after the bear and before the mouse.
- The mole went into the mitten after the mouse.
- The owl went into the mitten last.

B • The mouse went into the mitten first.
- The owl went into the mitten after the mouse.
- The mole went into the mitten after the owl.
- The rabbit went into the mitten after the mole.
- The bear went into the mitten last.

C • The rabbit went into the mitten first.
- The mole went into the mitten last.
- The mouse was the third animal to go into the mitten.
- The bear went into the mitten before the mouse.
- The owl went into the mitten after the mouse.

Animal Logic Problems *(cont.)*

These problems use five of the animal characters. *(cont.)*

D • The mouse went into the mitten last.

• The owl went into the mitten first.

• The rabbit went into the mitten third.

• The mole went into the mitten before the rabbit and after the owl.

• The bear went into the mitten before the mouse.

E • The mole went into the mitten first.

• The bear went into the mitten last.

• The owl went into the mitten before the bear.

• The mouse went into the mitten after the mole.

• The rabbit went into the mitten after the mouse and before the owl.

These problems use six of the animal characters.

A • The mouse went into the mitten first.

• The bear went into the mitten last.

• The mole went into the mitten third.

• The rabbit went into the mitten right after the mole.

• The owl went into the mitten before the mole.

• The fox went into the mitten before the bear.

B • The mole went into the mitten second.

• The fox went into the mitten before the mole.

• The mouse went into the mitten after the mole.

• The owl went into the mitten fifth.

• The rabbit went into the mitten before the owl.

• The bear went into the mitten after the owl.

C • The mole went into the mitten second.

• The fox went into the mitten fourth.

• The mouse went into the mitten sixth.

• The owl went into the mitten before the mole.

• The bear went into the mitten after the fox.

• The rabbit went into the mitten after the mole and before the fox.

D • The rabbit went into the mitten first.

• The bear went into the mitten two animals after the rabbit.

• The owl went into the mitten two animals after the bear.

• The fox went into the mitten after the rabbit.

• The mouse went into the mitten after the bear.

• The mole went into the mitten after the owl.

Animal Pictures for Patterns and Logic Problems

Teacher Note: See page 8 for directions to this activity.

Mouse	Mouse	Mouse	Mouse
Bear	Bear	Bear	Bear
Fox	Fox	Fox	Fox
Owl	Owl	Owl	Owl
Mole	Mole	Mole	Mole
Rabbit	Rabbit	Rabbit	Rabbit

Animal Pattern Pocket

Directions: Cut along the solid lines. Fold sides A and B back along the dashed lines so they meet at the back of the pocket. Tape the sides together. Tape the bottom of the pocket closed. Use the pocket to store your animal picture squares. (Fold the pocket flap inside the pocket to keep the pictures from falling out.)

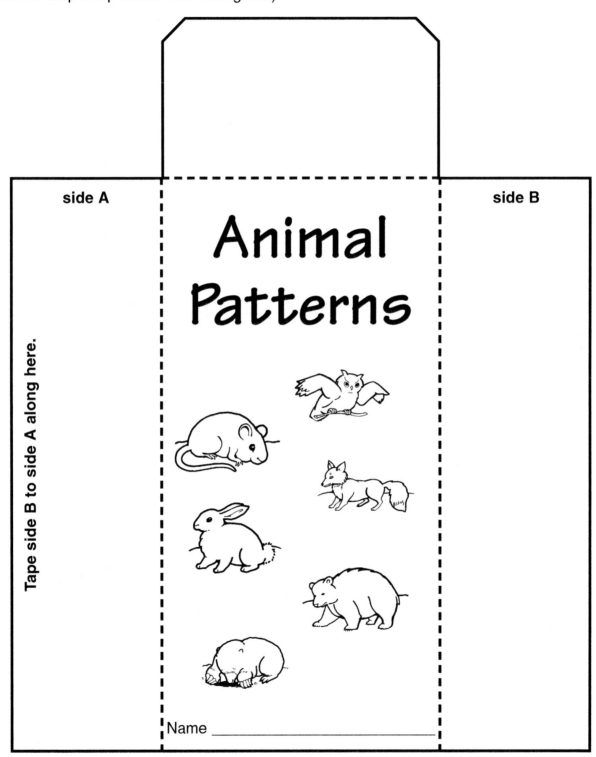

side A   side B

Tape side B to side A along here.

Animal Patterns

Name _____

Winter Days

_____
(Name of the Month)

Sunday	Monday	Tuesday	Wednesday	Thursday	Friday	Saturday
Mole	Rabbit					
			Hedgehog			Owl
		Badger		Fox	Bear	
Mouse						

Teacher Note: *Fill in the name of the month and the dates on the calendar.*

1. What is the name of the month on the calendar? _____

2. What day and date did Baba knit the mittens? _____

3. Name the animals that moved into the mitten during the second week of the month. _____

_____

4. Which three animals moved into the mitten during the same week? _____

_____

5. Which animal was third to move into the mitten? _____

6. How many animals moved into the mitten before the owl? _____

7. How many animals moved into the mitten after the owl? _____

8. What day of the week did Nicki have both of his mittens again? _____

9. Make addition and subtraction problems using the dates that fall on Saturday. (The date can be used as one of the numbers in the math problem or as the answer.) Write the equations on the back of this paper.

Mitten Math Activities

Numbers 0–12

Write the numbers 0–12 (or any other numbers that your class is studying) in scrambled order on the small mittens (page 38). Photocopy a set of the numbers for the class. Have the students color and cut out the mittens and glue them down in order on a piece of construction paper.

Numbers and Number Words

Write in selected numbers on the small left mittens (page 38) and the corresponding number in words on the small right mittens. Have the students color and cut out the mittens squares. Next, have them punch a hole in the corner of each mitten square. Tell them to tie a small piece of yarn to connect each number mitten to the mitten with its written form.

Calendar Math

Write numbers for your calendar on the small mittens (page 38). Photocopy the numbered mittens to use on the classroom calendar. Each day, have one of the students make a math problem for that day's date, using the numbers of that date as the answer or in the math problem. For example, for the 24th, the student might make an addition problem (2 + 4 = 6, 23 + 1 = 24), a subtraction problem (4 – 2 = 2, 25 – 1 = 24), a division problem (24 ÷ 6 = 4), etc.

Favorite Color of Mitten Graph

Give each student one of the large mittens (page 38). Tell them to color the mitten with their one favorite color. Make a giant graph out of the colored mittens on a piece of butcher paper. Generate questions and statements based upon the information shown on the graph. "How many students like red mittens?" "Six students like blue mittens." "Nobody likes yellow mittens."

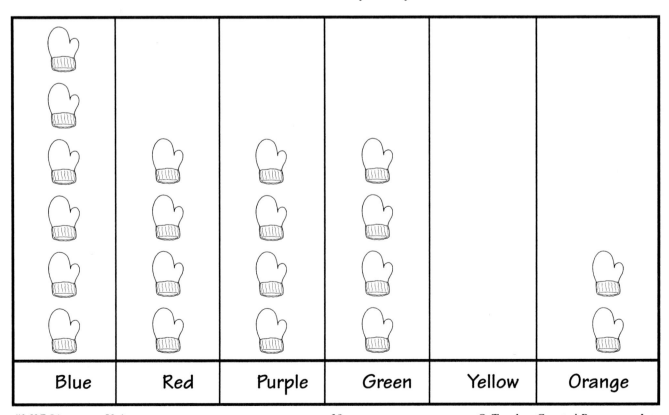

Blue	Red	Purple	Green	Yellow	Orange

Mitten Math Activities *(cont.)*

Mitten Math Problems

Use the small mittens (page 38) to make a math problem. Give each student two small mittens. They may color the mittens and then attach them to each other with strings or staples. Prepare a large piece of butcher paper for a mitten chart. Label the columns as shown below. Glue or staple each pair of mittens to the butcher paper as shown in the example.

Ask the students the following questions and record their answers on the butcher paper.

- How many pairs of mittens are in each row?
- How many single mittens are in each row?
- What math problems could you create out of the number of single mittens in each row?

Number of Mitten Pairs in Each Row	Total Number of Mittens in Each Row	Math Equations
1 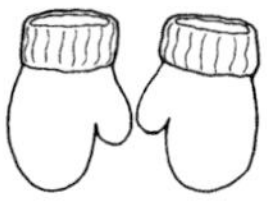	2	$1 + 1 = 2$ $0 + 2 = 2$ $2 + 0 = 2$ $2 - 0 = 2$
2 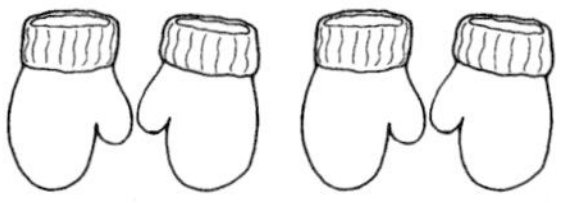	4	
3 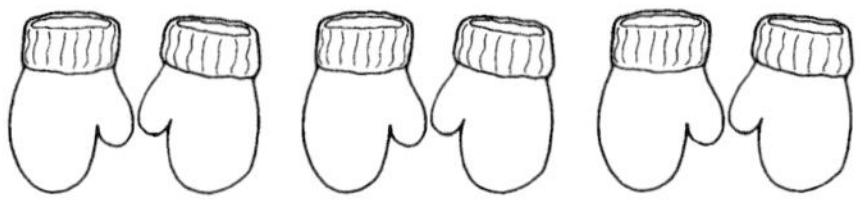	6	
4 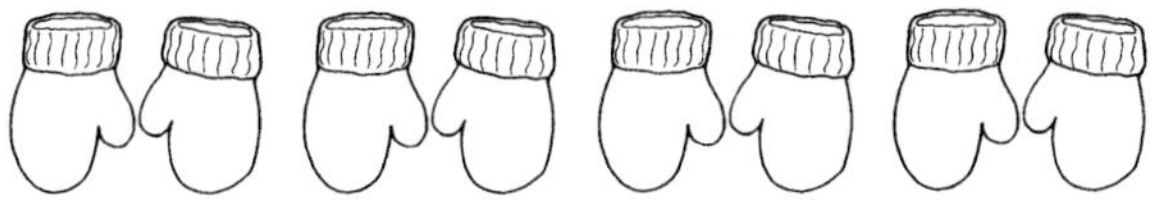	8	

Mitten Measuring *(Non-Standard Measurement)*

Make enlarged copies of the large mitten on page 38. Give each student one of these large mittens. Demonstrate how they may use their mittens (measuring end to end) to measure items around the classroom. Ask them to complete the activity on page 35.

Mitten Math Activities *(cont.)*

How Many Cubes Will Fit into Your Mitten? *(Non-Standard Volume)*

Make an enlarged copy of page 36 for each student. Ask the students how many multilinked cubes might fit inside of each mitten and tell them to write their estimates at the top of their papers. Then have them carefully fill their mittens, using multilinked cubes. Once the mittens are filled, they can then count how many cubes actually fit inside. This would make a great topic of discussion. Do all of the mittens hold the same number of cubes? Why would each mitten hold a different number of cubes? How close was your estimate?

To extend this activity, ask the students to bring real mittens to school. Tell them to estimate how many multilinked cubes it will take to fill the mittens and then ask them to fill the mittens. (Remind students not to force or overstuff cubes into the mittens.) How many cubes did it take? Why are there so many different answers? Did anyone come up with the same answer?

Mittens to 100

Make nine copies of page 38 and number the small mittens 0–100. Laminate the mittens and cut them apart. Have the students place the mittens in the pocket chart in the correct numerical order. Start small. Have the students place the mittens in order from 0 to 20. As the students become more proficient, add 10–20 more mittens at a time.

To extend this activity, give the students copies of the Mitten Number Board (page 37). Have them circle all of the numbers that end in five, all of the numbers you say when counting by 10, all of the odd (or even) numbers, numbers divisible by two, or numbers greater (or less) than 25, etc.

Before, in the Middle, and After

Make nine copies of page 38 and number the small mittens 0–100. (**Note:** Depending on the size of your pocket chart, you may wish to enlarge the patterns slightly.) Laminate the mittens and cut them apart. Place a series of numbers in the pocket chart in numerical order. Leave one number out (for example, 0, ___, 2, 3). Ask the students to tell you which number comes after 0, before 2, or in between 0 and 2. Have a volunteer place the appropriate number in the pocket chart. Repeat this activity several times. Each time use a different series of numbers.

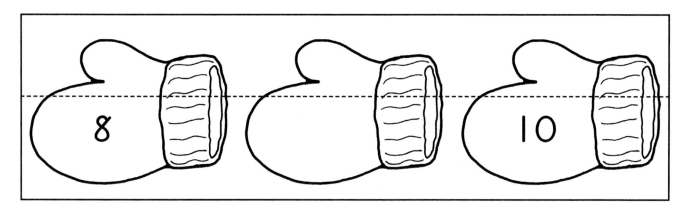

To extend this activity, give each student a copy of the Mitten Number Board (page 37). Think of a "mystery number" and give a clue to the students about it. For example: "Circle the number that comes before 38." The students should circle 37. Call on volunteers to give clues about their own "mystery numbers."

Mitten Math Activities *(cont.)*

Skip Counting by Twos, Fives, and Tens

Decide whether you wish to practice counting by twos, fives, or tens with the students. Make copies of the large mitten on page 38 and label them with the numbers that you deem necessary for this activity. For example, if you are going to be counting by twos, label the mittens 2, 4, 6, 8, 10, etc. Have several students come up in front of the class. Hand each student one of the numbered mittens. Have the students put themselves in order. Ask the entire class to chant the numbers in unison. As each number is said, have the student holding that number place it in the pocket chart.

To extend this activity, place selected numbers in the pocket chart. Then remove several of the numbers and have the students tell you which numbers are missing. Also, ask the students what the pattern is of the numbers in the pocket chart: twos, fives, or tens.

Challenge Activity: Place the numbers 0–20 in the pocket chart. Tell the students that you have a "secret number." Give the students clues to help them discover the secret number. For example, "The number is greater than 5 and less than 15. When you count by tens you say the secret number. What is the secret number?" *(Answer: 10)* More numbers can be added, and more challenging clues can be given as the students become more confident in working with numbers up to 100.

Pairs of Mittens

Give each student a copy of the large mitten on page 38. Tell them to color their mittens with their single favorite color. Ask the students how many pairs of mittens could be made out of all of the mittens in the class. What if each pair of mittens had to be the same color, how many pairs of mittens could be made? How many single mittens would be left over?

Numerical Order

Give each student a number. Ask the students to hold up their numbers so that they face out. Tell them to put themselves in numerical order without talking! This can be done several times with different sets of numbers.

Number Board to 100

Give each student a copy of the Mitten Number Board on page 37. Have the students color in the numbers used when counting by twos, fives, or tens. Ask the students what kind of pattern is made when the twos are colored in (or the fives or tens). Is it a column pattern? A checkerboard pattern? A stair-step pattern? A line pattern? At the bottom of the page, have the students each write a sentence to describe the pattern created.

1	2	3	4	5	6	7	8	9	10
11	12	13	14	15	16	17	18	19	20
21	22	23	24	25	26	27	28	29	30
31	32	33	34	35	36	37	38	39	40
41	42	43	44	45	46	47	48	49	50
51	52	53	54	55	56	57	58	59	60
61	62	63	64	65	66	67	68	69	70
71	72	73	74	75	76	77	78	79	80
81	82	83	84	85	86	87	88	89	90
91	92	93	94	95	96	97	98	99	100

Mitten Math Activities *(cont.)*

Number Puzzles

Photocopy the Mitten Number Board (page 37) onto different colors of paper and laminate them. For each number board, cut the numbers apart in different shapes to make a puzzle (see example below). Label the backs of the puzzle pieces with a letter (a different letter for each puzzle). This will make it easier to sort the pieces should several puzzles accidentally get mixed together. Place the pieces for each puzzle into a small envelope that has been labeled with the same letter on the outside. Give each student a puzzle. Have students put their puzzles together. (If a student is having difficulty, give him or her an intact Mitten Number Board to match the puzzle pieces to.)

To extend this activity, have the students create their own number puzzles. These can be traded with each other and solved.

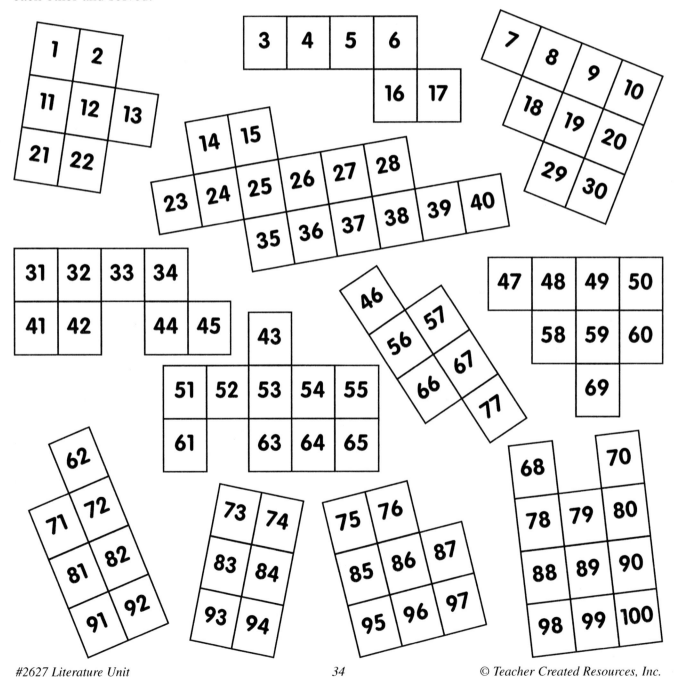

Mitten Measuring

Directions: Use your mitten to measure the following items. Record your findings.

My reading book is
_____ mittens long.

My desk at school is
_____ mittens long.

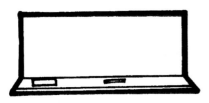

The chalkboard is
_____ mittens long.

The classroom bookcase is
_____ mittens wide.

My sharpened pencil is
_____ mittens long.

The classroom door is
_____ mittens tall.

How Many Cubes Will Fit into Your Mitten?

I think _____ cubes will fit into this mitten.

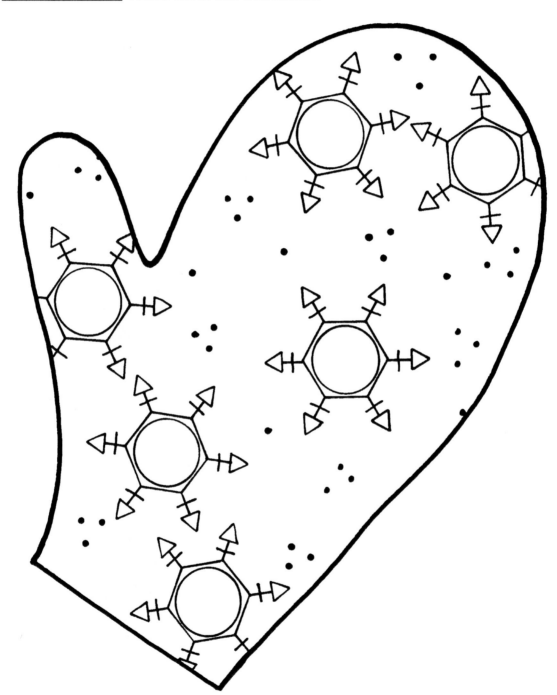

Challenge Activity: Figure out the difference between your estimated number and the actual number of cubes that fit into your mitten.

The difference is _____ cubes.

Mitten Number Board

See pages 32–34 for directions to this activity.

1	2	3	4	5	6	7	8	9	10
11	12	13	14	15	16	17	18	19	20
21	22	23	24	25	26	27	28	29	30
31	32	33	34	35	36	37	38	39	40
41	42	43	44	45	46	47	48	49	50
51	52	53	54	55	56	57	58	59	60
61	62	63	64	65	66	67	68	69	70
71	72	73	74	75	76	77	78	79	80
81	82	83	84	85	86	87	88	89	90
91	92	93	94	95	96	97	98	99	100

Mitten Patterns

See pages 36–38 for directions to this activity.

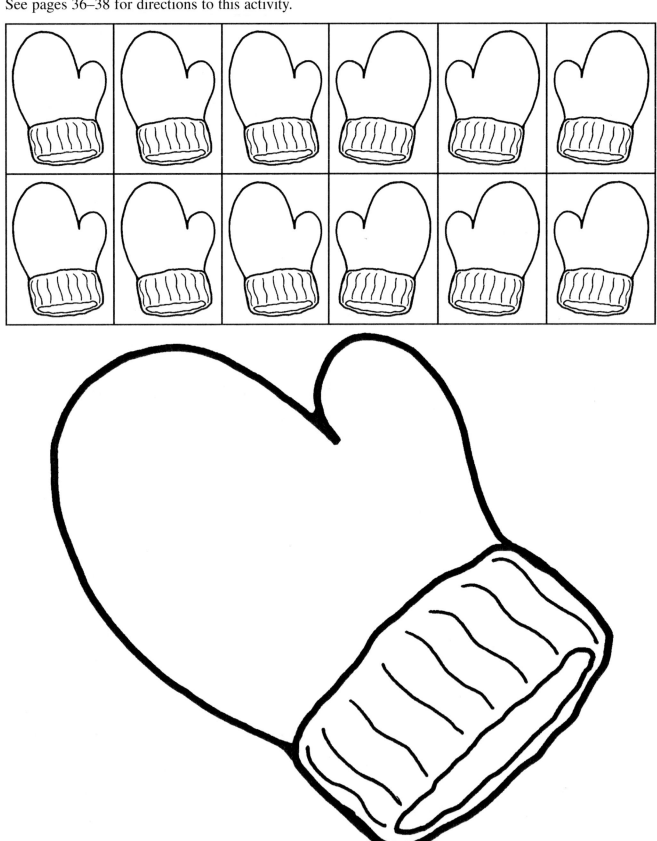

Ukraine

Ukraine is a European country slightly smaller in size than Texas. Ukraine means "borderland." This name is appropriate because Ukraine serves as a bridge connecting Europe with Asia. The capital of Ukraine is Kiev. There are more than 2.6 million people living in the capital city.

Ukraine is bordered by seven countries—Belarus, Russia, Moldova, Romania, Poland, Slovakia, and Hungary. There are two seas that border Ukraine—the Sea of Azov and the Black Sea. The Carpathian Mountains cut across the western border of Ukraine. The highest point is Mount Howverla at 6,762 feet (2,062 meters). The majority of the forest lands are located in the Carpathian Mountains. The Crimean Mountains are located in the southern end of Ukraine. The highest point is the Roman-Kosh Mountains at 5,059 feet (1,543 meters).

Ukraine has almost 23,000 rivers. One of the major rivers is the Dnepr River. It is 748 miles (1,204 km) long and runs through Ukraine.

Ukraine has a temperate climate and abundant natural resources. Ukraine has a strong agricultural base. The farmers grow grains, sugar beets, cotton, tobacco, grapes, potatoes, and other vegetables. Ukraine also has a strong fishing industry along the coasts of the Black Sea and the Sea of Azov.

Animals of Ukraine Follow-Up Questions

Teacher Directions: After the students have made their Animals of Ukraine books (pages 42–44), ask them the following questions:

- What are the two animals in the book that are not covered in fur? *(owl, hedgehog)*

- Which animal eats only meat? *(owl)*

- Which animal has prickly spines covering its body? *(hedgehog)*

- What are the three animals in the book that live underground in burrows and tunnels? *(mole, hedgehog, badger)*

- Which animal can fly? *(owl)*

- Which animals are nocturnal? *(owl, badger, fox, hedgehog, rabbit)*

- Which animal is a true hibernator? *(hedgehog)*

Map of Ukraine

Directions: Use the information below to fill in the map on the next page. Using a marker, write the names of the countries, rivers, mountain ranges, etc., on the map. Color each feature the appropriate color.

1. Russia borders the northeastern part of Ukraine. Color Russia red.

2. Belarus is directly north of Ukraine. Color Belarus orange.

3. Poland is northwest of Ukraine. Color Poland purple.

4. Slovakia is west of Ukraine and directly south of Poland. Color Slovakia pink.

5. Hungary is west of Ukraine and directly south of Slovakia. Color Hungary gray.

6. Romania is south of Ukraine and southeast of Hungary. Color Romania yellow.

7. Moldova is directly south of Ukraine. Color Moldova white.

Now finish filling in and coloring the rest of the map.

1. The capital of Ukraine is Kiev. Color the star yellow.

2. The Carpathian Mountains cut across the western part of Ukraine. Color the mountains brown.

3. The Crimean Mountains are located in the southernmost part of Ukraine. Color the Crimean Mountains brown.

4. The Black Sea washes up on the southern border of Ukraine. Color the Black Sea blue.

5. The Sea of Azov borders both Ukraine and Russia. Color the Sea of Azov blue.

6. The Dnepr River is 748 miles long and runs through Ukraine. Color the Dnepr River blue.

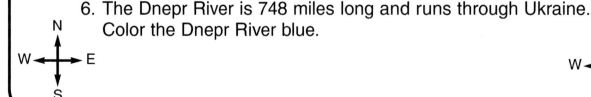

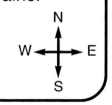

Map of Ukraine *(cont.)*

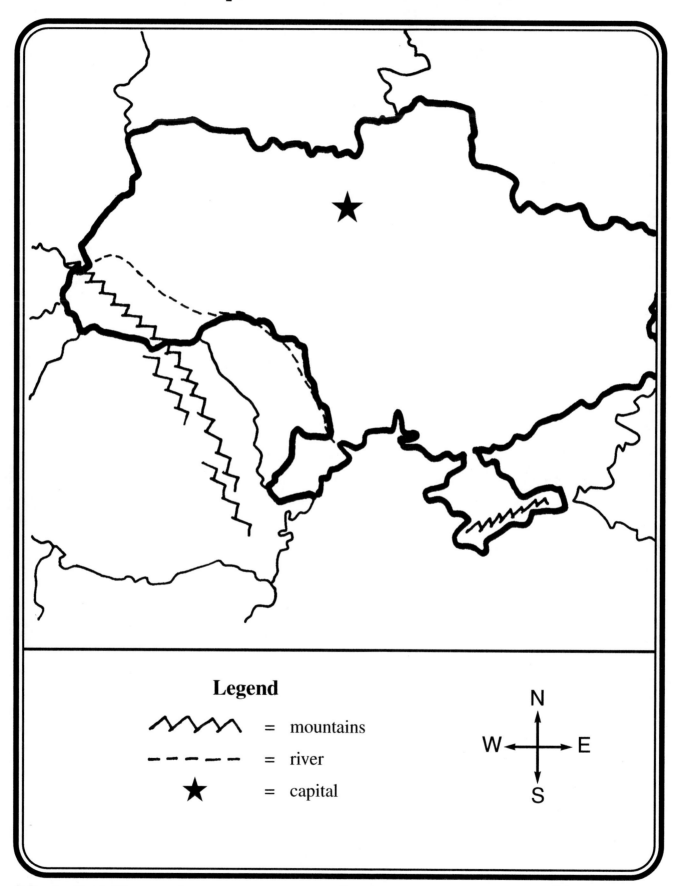

Legend

⋀⋀⋀⋀ = mountains

– – – – = river

★ = capital

N
W — E
S

Animals of Ukraine

Teacher Note: Directions for this activity are on page 9. Follow-up questions for after the activity are at the bottom of page 39.

Staple here.

Animals
of
Ukraine

Name:_____

Staple here.

Glue the correct animal picture from page 16 or 17 in this space.

Badgers have grayish-colored coats with black-and-white-striped patterns on their faces. Badgers are heavy and have short arms and legs, strong jaws, and large claws. They use their arms, legs, jaws, and claws to build their underground homes and to make escape routes. Badgers are nocturnal animals. They eat small animals like birds, frogs, and rats. Badgers also eat plants and honey.

Staple here.

Glue the correct animal picture from page 16 or 17 in this space.

The bear is a large, carnivorous mammal. Bears have poor eyesight but an excellent sense of smell. Bears can move quickly on both land and in the water. They are also very good tree climbers. Bears will eat just about anything—meat, vegetables, ants, honey, seeds, roots, berries, and nuts. Bears are not true hibernators. On warm winter days, a bear might wake up and come out of its den to look for food.

Animals of Ukraine *(cont.)*

Staple here.

Glue the correct animal picture from page 16 or 17 in this space.

The fox is related to the dog family. Foxes make their homes in burrows and sometimes in hollow stumps or rock crevices. The fox is nocturnal. During the day the fox hides, but at night the fox hunts for small birds, gophers, and rabbits. Sometimes, a fox will eat frogs, fish, insects, and berries.

Staple here.

Glue the correct animal picture from page 16 or 17 in this space.

The hedgehog is a small animal about the size of a rat. The spiny hedgehog rolls itself into a ball when it is frightened or attacked. The hedgehog is nocturnal. At night it pokes and digs into the ground, looking for insects, frogs, and other small animals to eat. During the winter, the hedgehog hibernates.

Staple here.

Glue the correct animal picture from page 16 or 17 in this space.

The meadow mouse has a very good sense of smell and hearing, but very poor eyesight. It has a small, fur-covered body and a long tail. The meadow mouse lives in fields, woodlands, and meadows. It eats nuts, berries, grasses, seeds, and insects.

Animals of Ukraine *(cont.)*

Staple here.

Glue the correct animal picture from page 16 or 17 in this space.

The mole is a small, fur-covered animal 3"–9" (8 cm–23 cm) long. Its tail can be as long as its body! It will spend most of its life in darkness. Quite often moles are blind due to skin that covers their eyes. The mole uses its shovel-like front feet to burrow and tunnel its way underground. The mole likes to eat earthworms and other small animals that do not have a backbone. The mole will often eat its weight in food each day. The mole does not hibernate during the winter.

Staple here.

Glue the correct animal picture from page 16 or 17 in this space.

Owls are nocturnal birds of prey. Owls have excellent hearing and nighttime vision. Their feathers allow them to fly soundlessly through the air. Owls like to eat small birds and rodents. Owls eat these animals whole and spit out the undigested parts in "pellets." The pellets are made up of the eaten animal's bones and fur.

Staple here.

Glue the correct animal picture from page 16 or 17 in this space.

The snowshoe rabbit is actually a hare. A hare is larger than a rabbit and has longer ears. The snowshoe rabbit is a gnawing animal, similar to rats, mice, and squirrels. At night they like to eat green growing things and rest during the day in their "form." A hare can run fast. When escaping from an enemy, it can stop and change directions very quickly. If necessary, the hare will fight off an enemy by kicking it with its strong hind legs, biting it, or even jumping over it!

Readers' Theater

A Readers' Theater Adaptation of *The Mitten*

Characters			
Narrator 1	Baba	Hedgehog	Fox
Narrator 2	Mole	Owl	Bear
Nicki	Rabbit	Badger	Mouse

Narrator 1: It's a cold winter day, and Baba is sitting by the fire with her knitting needles and a ball of yarn.

Nicki: Grandmother Baba, will you make a pair of mittens as white as snow for me?

Baba: Yes, Nicki, I will make a pair of mittens for you. But if I make white mittens, you will never find them if you drop them in the white snow. Why don't I make you a pair of red mittens?

Nicki: But Baba, I will not drop the mittens in the snow. Please make me a pair of snow-white mittens.

Baba: Okay, Nicki. I will make you a pair of mittens as white as the snow. However, every time you come home, I will check to make sure you are all right and then I will check to see if you have both of the mittens.

Narrator 2: So Nicki's grandmother made him a pair of mittens as white as the snow.

Narrator 1: The next day, Nicki went out into the snow-covered forest, wearing his white mittens. He didn't notice when he dropped one of them in the snow.

Mole: I am cold and tired from tunneling through the snow. I want to be warm.

Narrator 2: The mole saw the snow-white mitten and crawled inside it.

Mole: Ah, this mitten makes a nice home. I am warm and cozy. I think I will stay here.

Narrator 1: Along came a rabbit. He was cold from hopping around in the snow. The rabbit saw the mitten.

Rabbit: Mole, please let me come inside the mitten.

Mole: No, no! There is no room in here! Go away!

Narrator 2: But when the mole saw the rabbit's big kickers, he let him in. Soon the mole and rabbit were warm and cozy in the mitten.

Narrator 1: Along came a hedgehog. He was cold from snuffling around in the snow, looking for something to eat. The hedgehog saw the mitten.

Hedgehog: Mole and Rabbit, please let me come inside the mitten.

Mole and Rabbit: No, no! There is no room in here! Go away!

Narrator 2: But when the mole and rabbit saw the hedgehog's prickly spines, they let him in. Soon they were all warm and cozy in the mitten.

Narrator 1: Along came an owl. Owl saw all of the commotion going on inside of the mitten, and he swooped down to investigate.

Readers' Theater *(cont.)*

Owl: Mole, Rabbit, and Hedgehog, please let me come inside.

**Mole,
Rabbit, and
Hedgehog:**   No, no! There is no room in here! Go away!

Narrator 1:   But when the mole, rabbit, and hedgehog saw the owl's sharp talons, they let him in. Soon they were all warm and cozy in the mitten.

Narrator 2:   A badger popped up through the snow. The badger was cold from digging tunnels in the snow.

Badger: Mole, Rabbit, Hedgehog, and Owl, please let me come inside.

**Mole,
Rabbit,
Hedgehog,
and Owl:**   No, no! There is no room in here! Go away!

Narrator 1:   But when they saw the badger's diggers, they let him in. Soon they were all warm and cozy in the mitten.

Narrator 2:   The snow started to fall, and a fox was looking for someplace warm to stay. The fox saw the steam rising from the snow-white mitten.

Fox: Mole, Rabbit, Hedgehog, Owl, and Badger, please let me come inside.

**Mole,
Rabbit,
Hedgehog,
Owl, and
Badger:**   No, no! There is no room in here! Go away!

Narrator 1:   But when they saw the fox's shiny teeth, they let him in. Soon they were all warm and cozy in the mitten.

Narrator 2:   A great big bear saw the snow-white mitten and wanted to go inside to get out of the cold.

Bear: Mole, Rabbit, Hedgehog, Owl, Badger, and Fox, please let me come inside.

**Mole,
Rabbit,
Hedgehog,
Owl,
Badger, and
Fox:**   No, no! There is no room in here! Go away!

Narrator 1:   But the bear did not listen. He used his great size to push his way into the mitten. The mitten stretched to an enormous size, but Baba's knitting held fast. Soon they were warm, cozy, and squished inside the mitten.

Narrator 2:   Along came a small meadow mouse, looking for someplace to warm his body.

Mouse: Bear, may I sit upon your nose?

Readers' Theater (cont.)

Narrator 1:　Without waiting for an answer, the mouse climbed up on the bear's nose to get warm.

Narrator 2:　The mouse's furry body tickled the bear's nose. Without warning, the bear gave a gigantic sneeze, blowing all of the animals out of the mitten.

Narrator 1:　All of the animals quickly scurried away, leaving behind the snow-white mitten.

Narrator 2:　Nicki found his mitten laying on the ground. When he picked it up, he saw that the mitten had been stretched to an enormous size. Nicki walked home.

Baba:　Let me see if you are safe.

Narrator 1:　Baba looked Nicki over from head to toe and saw that he was safe.

Baba:　Let me see the mittens that I made for you that are as white as snow.

Narrator 2:　Nicki showed his grandmother both of the mittens. One of the mittens was small. The other mitten was very large.

Teacher Note: *The invitation below may be reproduced as is or enlarged. Send invitations to parents, family members, or even to other classes.*

You are cordially invited to attend

The Mitten

on _____ at _____

in _____.

We hope to see you there!

Bibliography

Other Books Written and Illustrated by Jan Brett

- *Annie and the Wild Animals.* Houghton-Mifflin, 1985.
- *Armadillo Rodeo.* G. P. Putnam's Sons, 1995.
- *Berlioz the Bear.* G. P. Putnam's Sons, 1991.
- *Christmas Trolls.* G. P. Putnam's Sons, 1993.
- *Comet's Nine Lives.* G. P. Putnam's Sons, 1996.
- *The First Dog.* Harcourt Brace Jovanovich, 1988.
- *Fritz and the Beautiful Horses.* Houghton-Mifflin, 1981.
- *The Hat.* G. P. Putnam's Sons, 1997.
- *Trouble with Trolls.* G. P. Putnam's Sons, 1992.
- *The Wild Christmas Reindeer.* G. P. Putnam's Sons, 1990.

Stories Retold and Illustrated by Jan Brett

- *Beauty and the Beast.* Clarion, 1989.
- *Goldilocks and the Three Bears.* G. P. Putnam's Sons, 1987.
- *The Mitten.* G. P. Putnam's Sons, 1989.
- *Town Mouse. Country Mouse.* G. P. Putnam's Sons, 1994.

Mitten-Themed Books

- Botting, Tom (translator). *The Mitten.* Malysh Publishers (USSR), 1975.
- Butterworth, Nick. *One Snowy Night.* Little, Brown and Co., 1989.
- Kellogg, Steven. *The Mystery of the Red Mitten.* Dial Books, 1974.
- Koopmans, Loek. *The Woodcutter's Mitten.* Crocodile Books, 1991.
- Michl, Reinhard. *Who's That Knocking at My Door?* Barron, 1986.
- Pollock, Yevonne. *The Old Man's Mitten: A Ukrainian Tale.* Mondo Publishing, 1975.
- Tresselt, Alvin R. *The Mitten.* Mulberry Books, 1964.

Related Nonfiction Books

- Hooper, Rosanne. *Life in the Woods.* Two-Can Publishing, Ltd., 1998.
- Mitchell, Sophie (editor). *Eyewitness Books: Mammal.* Alfred A. Knopf Inc., 1989.
- Potter, Tessa. *Digger: The Story of a Mole in the Fall.* Raintree/Steck-Vaughn, 1988.
- Royston, Angela. *Eyeopeners: Birds.* MacMillan Publishing Co., 1992.
- *Scholastic First Discovery Book: Under the Ground.* Editions Gallimard, 1990.

Related Fiction Books

- Bodnar, Judit Z. *Tale of a Tail.* Lothrop Lee and Shepard Books, 1998.
- Ehlert, Lois. *Mole's Hill.* Harcourt Brace and Co., 1994.
- Waddell, Martin. *The Happy Hedgehog Band.* Candlewick Press, 1994.
- Waddell, Martin. *Mimi and the Dream House.* Candlewick Press, 1995.
- Yolen, Jane. *Eeny, Meeny, Miney Mole.* Voyager Picture Books, 1996.

Software

- *Travel the World with Timmy.* Software. Edmark. P.O. Box 97021, Redmond, WA 98073-9721. (1-800-691-2986). Win/Mac CD-ROM.
- *Trudy's Time and Place.* Software. Edmark. P.O. Box 97021, Redmond, WA 98073-9721. (1-800-691-2986). Win/Mac CD-ROM.
- *The Tree House.* Software. Bröderbund. 500 Redwood Blvd., Novato, CA 94948. (1-800-548-1798). Win/Mac CD-ROM.
- *Carmen Sandiego Junior Detective Edition.* Software. Bröderbund. 500 Redwood Blvd., Novato, CA 94948. (1-800-548-1798). Win/Mac CD-ROM.

Videotapes

- *Eyewitness: Bear.* Dorling Kindersley Limited, 1997. (35 minutes)
- *Really Wild Animals: Awesome Animal Builders.* National Geographic, 1997. (46 minutes)